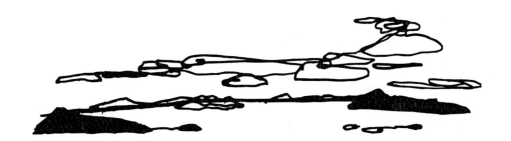

NIGHT LUNCH

Mike Chaulk

Copyright © 2020 Mike Chaulk.

All rights reserved. No part of this work may be reproduced or used in any form, except brief passages in reviews, without prior written permission of the publisher.

Cover photograph by Mike Chaulk
Cover design by Jeremy Luke Hill
Interior illustration by Devon Sioui
Book design by Jeremy Luke Hill
Set in Athelas
Printed on Mohawk Via Felt
Printed and bound by Arkay Design & Print

LIBRARY AND ARCHIVES CANADA CATALOGUING IN PUBLICATION

Title: Night lunch / Mike Chaulk.
Names: Chaulk, Mike, 1989- author.
Description: Poems.
Identifiers: Canadiana (print) 20190225351 | Canadiana (ebook) 2019022536X |
    ISBN 9781928171942 (softcover) | ISBN 9781928171959 (PDF) |
    ISBN 9781928171966 (HTML)
Classification: LCC PS8606.H3927 N54 2020 | DDC C811/.6—dc23

Gordon Hill Press respectfully acknowledges the ancestral homelands of the Attawandaron, Anishinaabe, Haudenosaunee, and Metis Peoples, and recognizes that we are situated on Treaty 3 territory, the traditional territory of Mississaugas of the Credit First Nation.

Gordon Hill Press also recognizes and supports the diverse persons who make up its community, regardless of race, age, culture, ability, ethnicity, nationality, gender identity and expression, sexual orientation, marital status, religious affiliation, and socioeconomic status.

Gordon Hill Press
130 Dublin Street North
Guelph, Ontario, Canada
N1H 4N4
www.gordonhillpress.com

For my father, Brent Chaulk

NIGHT LUNCH

*It is undone business
I speak of, this morning,
with the sea
stretching out
from my feet*

— Charles Olson "Maximus, To Himself", *The Maximus Poems*

// **I**

I await, still, my great white-bear
who heavy brave against a long slag north

with the ice, chose fair this ex-barren bloom,
chose me, the young seaman who's not yet seen.

Cape Harrison haunts, throws foam ghosts against
its bluffs, crashes white bears that fall back to

waves: sick boasts of the one not sighted, mine,
its eyes the colours of whole milk and grease.

I set a wide stance to Harrison's swell,
emblazon binoculars on my eyes

that, allied to nausea's sick-billowed tide,
breaks siege on three pasted Purity crackers—

and this, of Labrador, unlike, appears;
I await, still, my great white-bear.

//   2

Another sleep given the backbreaker
by Lester, the booming Inuk deckhand
who says I have a French poodle haircut;
a shaky few hours pulled from sweet deepest.

Half hour to Hopedale my light, perked, smothers;
I whisper fuck you to everyone I've
ever known, dress two pants, hoodie, two coats,
coveralls, a hardhat, steeled boots, gloves still wet.

On deck, cold cuts dark and fills bones to seize,
snowy barrens, clenched muscles pushed to flake
the spring line to fairlead, tie a heaving line.
Two more cleaved 'hands show, grunt, climb to the bow.

Ducked in the fo'c'sle, I rest on boxed freight,
fucked shoulder shaking like cable over weight.

// 3

Waiting to be overtaken and so then never,
a rock stays course under its waterfall's

sustained assault, weaker for all the years,
smaller for, as age and people your age—

the deckhand on watch pounds, *half hour!*
I wake into night unimpressed, I gear

more often than dress: an athlete of sorts.
Freight off, back now bunked with questions, again.

For the barrens, our lost gravestones, white-bear,
forgetting yaw that howls like wind through

a tear in taut plastic. And best sleep then,
best hidden, caved in music from high school.

But wind dies like days and the plastic sleeps.
Wake needs a ship yet is its own, complete.

// 4

I fly with my father over the bush,
stare out through the cutting, doomed propeller.
He, newly nineteen and fox-furred in that
red Beaver, eats a bologna sandwich.

A face like mine from a photographed age,
the sky bent sepia, my grandmother,
whose lungs still speak praises of Labrador
in winter, rubs her worry-stones smooth flat.

There are times, this, when duress grows a pen:
the engine gulps thick, stops, and young father
looks out to where my cloud-shaped mother,
his future, births chains of bright years, and me.

Uteral quiet, steel whale among clouds,
he reels through to me: *This isn't allowed.*

// 5

He farts in the shower six feet from where
I sleep, a man who has shared so much time
every sound builds scenes. I know his supper,
his defaulted face through rung Crosby hooks,

his face torn from sleep into this racket,
demented in away and middle-aged.
His family, their smartphones, their rates and dreams
increasingly similar to mine: gutted.

Awakened hateful hours before my watch,
grip's still Harrison's, whose reach and leaves slow
like the foothills' roll after the tallest.
God is a tablecloth-swiping trick, if—

the boat pitches, stands him six feet above;
I dog-dig in my eyelids, desperate for off.

// **6**

Wake up young feller! Light pounds into place,
kicks the door in on a far shipless dream.
Windy enough to blow the dick off ya!
The ship's motion, unhinged, swells in my guts.

Thirsts a heady hate, shameful, born into
the best air I've breathed behind nausea
shared with my white-bear. The Labrador Sea
rolls us starboard, pulls skulls with blood tidal,

then sends us hard port, forcing groans through steel.
These winds kill our speed, make for a long watch
while our own weathers, topographical,
drag up the map's coast.   Not in any mood.

The gyro reader clicks steady countdown.
Mate: *Ever tell ya 'bout how I flip cars?*

// 7

It can happen to anybody sure,
skipper says, calm through a white captain's beard.

I know guys who've been at it all their lives
that still fall over sick. Not the best life.

We laugh about it now while seas ease slight
toward Makkovik, recent sightings of bears.

Lee is a light word, seems furthest from where
I wished bergs against our mortal hull.

Worst, I admit, but hours of worse pitching;
heavy steel dropping under, rose buoyant,

forced me three times the bridge wing's fresh frigid,
a wind-flat t shirt.   —I squeezed out my guts.

Each time, came back in, said, *Okay, better,*
scoria-flecked skin tight like cold leather.

// **8**

Let us comfort. I remember mothers
hiding chicken bones in the school sandbox,

mine so laughing, strong, a bright windbreaker.
She moves tight in her skin—taller, eyes priding.

Someone I squeeze so hard my fears away,
spinning like a star-nosed mole blind happy,

finally that palaeontologist.
Tower in the role to impress this Lauren.

    Green suburbs empty every morning and
    years later, I trespassed that ghost-quiet.

    Things lost weight: houses pulled at their basements,
    tried hardest not to fall into the sky—

Shh, there for a moment, we stand like poles,
backs to the mothers placing bones in holes.

// **9**   *for Norman Dugal*

There's a photo of my mother's father
in uniform on deck a navy ship,
heavy painted steel and sky behind him.

Never spoke about our shared work, the sea,
but wonder if a connection is forged
by how the sound of the engine room enwombs;

of early watches, down hatches, night lunch,
the black hellish smell of bilge to our boots,
the bulkheads creaking us to sleep in swell.

I learned this trick to keep from rolling off
a bunk here, Poppy: wedge a lifejacket under
your weight and lay pressed to the bulkhead—though

I'm sure you know, and even I'll pretend
you taught me or, through generations, sent.

// **10**

Maximus climbs the gangway, never leaves,
pins an old, worn prayer card to the bulkhead above

our bunks. I found it in a desk drawer on
another ship last crewed by Polish men.

*Our Lady Star of the Sea, for all those
who came before us,* he says, *a good measure.*

*To those who slept in these bunks before us,
and if naught else,* he boasts, *the finest scene.*

He comes and goes often, Maximus does,
as if we were on different watches, brings

me rocks, old bones, a shoe he found ashore.
All come with stories: our kin, those before,

can't you feel them? At our porthole he stands
for those who claimed land: *I hunt among stones.*

// II

Now he sleeps, snores heaving like a father
on the top bunk above mine. He exhales
full heavy fogs, each tuned to the slightest
sea swell. There: an old humpback, his belly.

Steel hinges bend on their bolts under him,
swear weight while he mouths past centuries. Squints.
Ships wrecked in the creases of his forehead,
full of survivors. What of survivors

here? Lockwood School in Cartwright, the Makkovik
Boarding School, Nain Boarding School, St. Anthony
Orphanage and Boarding School, Yale School
in Northwest River. Culture scourged. Language—

he wakes and sweats: *I dreamt I was nothing.*
Big guy, me too, I say, red-eyed, writing.

// **12**

Big old Max always speaking of ghosts. Bent,
he tracks their walks across these barrens, their

catalogue of supplies: food, fuel, surnames
always settling on arrival, first foot

on fresh stone like a deep breath of cleanest
arrogance, as if untouched, unpeopled,

a full body stretch, a *Get to work, men,*
attitude which is to say, *This is ours.*

How many ghosts abreast are mine, split down
a family washed through of settlers come

and those colonized both—of Inuit,
Cree, of Chaulk Lake. How it was claimed, named.

How many of them are mine? Are all? None?
Should I drift off, born-out, unpeopled, null?

// **13**

The ship steams abreast distant Mokami
mountain from the hills like a minke's fin.

At long last, a few hours out of Goose Bay,
it greets week-dead cellphones; signals newly

proliferate, refract into heavens;
a sick angel wakes, breaks into gold beams

and somersaults across the waters,
Lake Melville, to land.   *—How was that trip North?*

My mom's voice calms, asks where we're at now.
Same mountain, same deck filled with folks on phones

laugh. *Your sister Jen and your dad danced to
the song "Old Mokami" at Jen's wedding,*

she reminds me.   And in a way, we are too;
Mokami glints; we dance a three-way, new.

// 14

I can't sleep when the main engines are off.
Quiet falls only two docked nights each week
and lets in the house-sounds. Bulkheads whimper,

the hum of air circulation systems
usually drowned in our storm of machine-
purpose. The hammer of one oiler

against one part, some steel pipe or another,
destroys an image I hold dearly:
our entire engine-room crew swarming

the two engines, climbing them all over
like remora fish to a great, vital shark.
Running ships give work, a place to stay, food.

But I've seen a ship leak, a ship with fires,
seen crews on TV remembered with choirs.

// 15

Comes through the thin bulkhead a strange new noise,
bleating its time, a sharp waltz of drawn notes

lifts in me a feeling of something on
something dredged over from my other life—

Saturday Night's friends next morning
cook in the kitchen together something

golden: market bacon, fresh bread,
a dozen eggs—and draws me out for a snack.

Loud through his open door, the bosun
sits on his bunk squeezing an accordion.

*Thoughts I would try at it couple a years
ago, sure as Jesus not very good.*

He chugs a half can of Rockstar from Nain.
Steve knocks, *sup b'ys*, and the jig starts again.

// **16**

Just a couple Coors Light left in the fridge
he brought from Corner Brook, the bosun throws

a cold one to each of us. A beauty
day untied from Goose Bay, an easiest

Lake Melville shows no threat or swell.
Best to stay up now and wait for supper.

What's Cooky cookin' up for us tonight?
Bologna stew, I say, a joke that lands

because last week it poured pink into our bowls,
thick-cut straight off the Maple Leaf Big Stick.

Plus carrots, onions, potatoes pepto.
Terry hears talk through the bulkheads, comes in,

   Anyone know what's for supper the'night?

Lord Jesus you're not hungry already!

// **17**

Hockey Night in Canada fills the ship
through. Updaters call up to the wheelhouse.
Groggy oilers stride by the lounge door. Their heads,
angled, reappear until the score's heard.

This creates talk across generations,
a shared language to pass long night watches.
    Where's that old Michael Ryder to now?
    New Jersey. With Clowe, a line fed by Jiggs.

In the hold, Terry knows who owns one shipment.
His kind. He sharpies the Habs' crest. *Le buuuuuuuuut!*
he writes. Then, next trip, a Sundin-painted
komatik's brought on. *S'good firewood here, b'ys!*

A tether ashore, connection to homes; wharfingers
chirp before the heaving line's even thrown.

// **18**

When crisis cracks, *The Young and the Restless*
moves through the ship like a slow potent wind.

*Did you hear what happened on the news
today?* Terry might say, up the wheelhouse

for a yarn. Even men you'd think never,
say, *Oh you don't say, no shit, really?*

Say, *The missus watched it for years, got hooked
at some time or other not half bad though.*

Another, on watch at air time, hand up:
You Jesus best not repeat a damn thing.

I'm on reruns, he says, rushing down his
supper and quick to the ship's one armchair,

eager to keep up with the crew's gossips
and leave his body abreast for a minute.

// 19

The way an empty hall flutters: a yawn
scatters thin, eddies up quiet dust.
I refill my skin. Pushed edges bend and

dreams bead off into my windshield's drain.
I could have been revived, speaking of lands
through a rare absence of the 'hand on watch

who unleashes the sprung racket of work
into slept life, again: the rolling steel
wool cumulus who kicks in, grates with light:

scoured wonder, clean. Even barrens hold lichen,
and puffins speak into each others' tongues
of night. I enter to never know of mine

without another to ask what was dreamt.
Cracked knuckles pushed to my eyes, I forget.

// **20**

Who is to blame that he has
never once been to a planetarium?
Though that that doesn't hurt him
the way he writes it might.

That he has never lost somebody
close, never knelt, bowed,
or been knighted in the use of *agony,*
which forces the third person.

If, even now,
on a ship long in deep swell,
he is not uncomfortable, can read,
then another hardship poem remains

unfinished.
People your age die all the time.

// **21**

The horn blasts set intervals through dense fog
and falls back flat into slow black swell, holds
our young deckhand asleep in his bunk

and allows time for us now to cross-section.
A ship's demons circle over-under,
drip the sea off, plunge, upward, in turn.

Their numbers grow with the crew, mobs of haunts
along with—   their teeth drip error and sea
dark as the blood of addiction, the pasts

of loved ones that are dreamt and stay days.
Some seamen don't dream at sea, old tales say
and when ashore, they only dream of the sea.

So grows their ghosts, their pain-courting hecklers,
burning like lit fossils in shallow ground.

// 22

Example: Dale before discharge.
His sand-grain pupils, small to near sea-black,
push from their outermost convex and beg
away from a high-tide of opiates.

His back is *Gahn,* he said. Forty long years
workin' like a dog and an accident
to add, *young feller,* impaled by rebar
or almost. *Never been the same*; all pain.

One time they couldn't wake him from his door,
calling in, half hour from tie up. Worried now.
So they shook him til he sprung, stood torqued,
still in his ripped coat: a jet over his heart.

Dale smoked cartons, drank a bay of coffee;
he taught me to splice in the fo'c'sle ably.

// **23**

Most I know of Fogo is it found them
too, as it does, and lowers all to the deck.
Our third mate stood ghost on Nain's dock, wharf phone
at his head says, *No, no but*   —his brother.

His niece upstairs drying clean hair when he
did it, shotgun pushed against his forehead:
cold steel. The wall behind him. Next flight to   —ghost.
The charter plane's called and we leave him.

All that continues crushed into margins
by a named vacuum that—   *He was*—   throbs blue
in its explosive birth against grown skies,
thrown perspectives, the Great Big where behind close,

unspinning alone in no centre there:
his niece in the mirror drying her hair.

// **24**

The next star in a constellation of loss, of gones
forever pieces overhead a likeness,
an image still being wrought, overflows
names. Too inhabitable under broke time.

Similarly, some crew on deck leans over
the bulwark, unable to sleep. We watch
how Borealis disappoints tonight,
flails thin, a green cord missing its socket.

Each hand points over all different barrens
toward their configurations. We fall hardest into   when—
how its ancient slide across deep sky
drives a star through morning, holds it below.

Settling near, their geometry is new;
slowly, it begins taking after you.

// **25**

Terry opens Darren's cabin door slow.
Darren wakes barely, his thin hair matted

from a fogged nap. He leans in, asks him
if he's goin' down for hot Sunday Dinner.

Like a kid asked through a deep fort, Darren
says *No, too tired*   —no better than away.

Later Darren comes out on deck to us
saying he just about died when he wokes,

saying, *I jesus knows who done it too,*
that goddamn Terry, who cranked his thermostat

til he woke up drowned in sweat. *Couldn't breathe*
sure. Holy livin' jesus in hell, boys.

From the bow, Terry yells out, *How's your nap?,*
then laughs 'til he cries beneath his hardhat.

//   26

Rich is early at the dock, having danced
all night. Still drunk, but able to tie us up.
It's a goddamn miracle, he says, and tears
off in his forklift, humming last call tunes.

Cartwright sleeps by the bay, smells of wood stoves,
folks asleep. Fog against heated windows.
Rare free time in the town, my grandmother's
own when young, of her family's past   —mine.

So I walk past the fish plant in coveralls
toward the old graveyard where I might find them.
Captain Cartwright, the town's namesake, whose book
of journals I brought from my father's shelf,

has a memorial built for him here.
I guess up a hill, smell smoking fish in the wind.

//   27

Broken redberries and Labrador tea
force a shrunken path between worn graves.
—*who departed this life* carved into so many.
An old convention, all dead centuries here.

The Captain's marble cairn in the corner looks
out the bay, spotted with blood-red lichen.
Sent over here from England. A land he loved
and claimed by name, or else named for later.

I'm unsure. A spider crawls up one urn,
checked by a wind sent through the quiet morning.
But the cairn is broken, its back half gone
so long that moss attempts its hollow too.

I read the words carved for him on high ground
complicate: a friend to people then, but—

// **28**

*IN MEMORY OF GEORGE CARTWRIGHT, CAPTAIN
OF HIS MAJESTY'S 37th REG.
OF FOOT, SECOND SON OF WILLIAM CARTWRIGHT
ESQre OF MARNHEN HALL ... NOTTINGHAMSHIRE*

*WHO IN MARCH 1770 MADE
A SETTLEMENT ON THE COAST OF LABRADOR
WHERE HE REMAINED FOR SIXTEEN YEARS.   HE DIED
[IN ENGLAND]... FEBRUARY 1819.*

*TO THESE DISTINGUISHED BROTHERS, WHO
IN ZEALOUS PROTECTING AND BEFRIENDING,
PAVED THE WAY FOR THE INTRODUCTION
OF CHRISTIANITY TO THE NATIVES*

*IN THESE BENIGHTED REGIONS. THIS ... INSCRIBED
BY THEIR NIECE FRANCES DOROTHY CARTWRIGHT*

// 29

Cartwright agonizes, shaking by the fire
alone. I read so. It was out Sandwich Bay,
he was ill. But when docked near there
this morning, I don't feel him.

Max shakes his head at me. I climb too easy
away. *Always have, big guy. My very worst*
thought is that I need someone dearest
to die. No choice then but to, against death, try.

A broken salmon circles the surface
off the wharf, breaks stillness, begging to be
hooked near where Charles, Cartwright's friend, no marksman,
missed a shot and killed his dog.   He left him

in the bush with the bullet and broke down.
Hopeless, Charles sickened, would never find ground.

// **30**

Cartwright, old man, your people are dying:
Poor Charles of sickness, still dogless, bled by
you at his bedside and stored frozen in snow
until the thawed land allowed burial.

(never). Then Ickeuna, May 31,
1773, of disease
from London; her sister Caubvick you shaved
bald, her hair you locked away in a trunk.

You assumed it harboured disease—never you.
Their village screamed all night, dug into hills.
      Today, news of two men drowned in Cartwright.
      Drunk. One dove in to save his friend who fell.

That longliner's theirs, I'm told. It floats on.
I wonder how you felt your role in it all.

// **31**

He overlooks a second graveyard, down
the bottom of a dirt slope toward the shore,
lie those gone before us, some newly they—
body-long rounds of dirt like tanning beds,   or—

Closer the shore the larger the gravel,
hard and heavy; no cranberries or tea,
padded steps, no time for moss to thicken.
THESE BENIGHTED REGIONS. Tall grass and hogweed.

Here are more recent deaths, dates, names of less
fortune, many written on white-painted
wood crosses with permanent marker, fade.
A white-bear painted next a Union Jack.

The half-hour horn blows, claiming all ashore.
I forget my grandmother's maiden name.

//   **32**

At the foot of a barren, Maximus
calls to me, bows now like a tongue unfolds.
He repeats. Sandwich Bay falls from his eyes.
Then he stands, lists, taller than a mast,

two men wide, and points over the barren.
Captain Cartwright hunts on the other side,
Max says, *he found a baby seal*
and laughs mercy at its acrobatics.

Come, he begs, burying his balding head
between two padded, lichen-wet palms,
obsessed with a man centuries past skeleton.
His ribs a braying horse's long, slow fall.

Big Guy, I'm done, I say. Why claim him mine?
Rich, let go of the spring-line.
                                                   Please.

// 33

In memory of Caubvick, of Ickeuna,
who left Labrador in Fall 1772
with Cartwright; afraid
as home distanced, they studied maps and charts.

After the opera and dinner parties,
paraded for whites, the group boarded for home
from London's slums.
The four fell sick, all the Inuit. Stomachs.

Ickeuna died, he wrote. *Attuiock died.*
His wife, Ickcongoque, Ickeuna's
mother, died sometime too.
Caubvick returned, silent, shaved, and alone.

Some family grabbed rocks, bashed their own faces.
Cartwright cried but wrote them out as traces.

// **34**

Sonny, stout Inuit man from Postville, sits
across me first meal out, tells a story
of a white-bear, nanuk, he hunted,

chosen for his community's quota.
He showed photos, splayed flat white on his shed floor,
worth lots but he'll never sell. We'd talk through

suppers. Once, slow through Eskimo Passage,
land close, lichened in blurs, Sonny comes
on deck and asks, *So you got some Inuit?*

I stutter out, *Some yeah don't know
how much my dad's from Goose. Some Cree
from round there too—* He leans serious, says,

*Listen here, it don't work that way. If you
got blood, you got it.   Plus you looks it too.*

// **35**

My dad tells this one story of firsts,
of the time, not so young, he learned

the taste of watermelon, of how kids
would chase the shipment through Northwest River,

dirt clouds ripping off tires along the bridge
to hard Sheshatshiu, an Innu reserve.

He calls it the best thing he's ever had,
a new taste paramount. *Some good. Juicy.*

Must have come by boat, as we do now, carrying
goods north through ice. Working without break

I bounce off of the things I can never know:
felt treaties, stricken love, a rooted pride.

With a mix of bloods, I work up the coast.
The crew prefers toast to watermelon.

// **36**

Thirty minutes there young feller, wake up!
Light makes lucid the world like a new slide
from a projector I'm still stuck inside.
My sheet, stressed from its mattress tuck,
forces my bare skin to the fibrous bunk,
decades old. Sore feet forced into wet boots
and on the steel deck, alone, lightless black
swell, the ship lists. I brace against a rail,
shift with full motion toward the fo'c'sle, dogged.
The moon's hung high, bright like presence to pray to.
We roll slight starboard, hard port, then plunge,
pushing heavy sea-spray over me, salt

in the gasp I make: I can't be out here.
I was wrong.
                        I should be up at the wheel.

// **37**

Gather 'round now, crew, the night lunch cold plate:
turkey, ham, iridescent roast beef splash

colours, rolled loose: spokes of a perfect circle;
cubed orange cheddar, white mozz piles the centre,

scatter of gherkins form the foothills, O.
Cooky's long asleep after the midnight

watch change; port to stern deck open, smokers
eye the white wake bloom from blackness; moon out.

One rolls one tube and disappears it;
one, shaker close, salts each slice of wet ham;

one tells a story through cheese-pasted teeth;
one crafts with slow care a sandwich, white bread,

forgetting a moment the nitrate pool
on the plate, and listens—together—speaks.

// **38**

Again, Maximus speaks of those long gone,
brushes their footfall like fossils, cherished;

eyes to the gravel, back to those whose feet
fall now, whose gait has been long impacted

by those men treasured more, their arrival.
I hear a voice call out, *Get to work, boys!*

and wonder how much my work here extends
from a settler history built to displace.

Captain Rogers, though beloved, is white.
Some crew call Natuashish Nutville and laugh.

I came here to work, connect; to remember.
You bend and kiss beginnings to forget

this land long loud with footsteps, family, trade routes;
my family line bruised with long forgetting too.

// 39

I used to fear the old basement bearskin.
Concealed behind black coats from cornered beams
it hung whitely. A terrible pink gaped out
a teeth-stretched snout, hard to small-knuckled knocks.

Then one day it was gone. A new wall glared.
A new pink: insulation through thick plastic.
After asking where it ever went to,
I was told it had never been a bear.

It was an arctic wolf, my mom tells me.
My sister would pull it out, lay on it
but dad, one time lifted by rum, gave it
to his best friend Dave's then brother in law

who wore it through the airport on his back,
a dark stripe running down its flattened length.

// **40**

Some time on the ship now, my language trawls
first-learned inflections, born Maritimer:
half Labradorian in Halifax—some young.
Long-corrected vowels revert, sing.

Where's you from? Grew up in Guelph, but my old man's
from Goose Bay and most his friends Newfoundlanders
like the crew. Long calls, loud laughs through the house,
holiday dinners. I learned this speech early.

Five months in now and full as an egg with it,
though I still keep the o in boys for the b'ys
so as not to overstep, taunting their
Bud Lights, ubiquitous, over card games.

All my life my language was tinted, called off.
Here now, surrounded, it swells—given breath.

// 41

*Jiggs is some good, cook!—used to hunt. They built
the road near me, cut—on the news last night?
Phyllis still coma—I'll do it after
dinner here—shouldn't be allowed, shouldn't—
That fishing racket's not for me, boys, nope,
eighteen hours, all night and day—salt beef—
Not that old* Young and the Restless *again—
A fisherman works without reference to
that difference—you sleeps stood up, gets used to it—
busier than a dog with six dicks—thinking
offshore, enough of this;—fish farms? The shit—
First men in it, the leaders, explorers
were WORKERS—How bout them Habs last night, eh?—
You sick fucker, there's something wrong with you.*

//   **42**

Up in the bridge for a yarn, I relieve
the deckhand on watch for dinner and look
about for whales. Chart's changed, I scan closely,
read a Sweethome Island off starboard.

Someone named it, thinking it was theirs to,
missed so much their own, as I do, near halved
between finding home here and all my other life.
I shake it off. It's easy to forget

these charts, a history in themselves, displace
the names held before the homesick arrived.
Another White Bear Island. *Lot of those,*
first mate says, *I know one's out Groswater.*

Lot of those, islands named for white bears seen,
that ghost now the north with translated name.

// **43**

In Nain, on dock for my last time this season,
Lester points to the cliff face where the bay meets
Mt. Sophie. *See the nanuk? Polar bear.*
In the mountain there, that white marking.

That nanuk in the hill was created
years ago when a bear approached some kids
playing. The village Shaman seen the bear
and cast a spell to trap it there—to guard.

When sun's a certain way, the nanuk shines,
ancient on dark granite overlooking. Is this
the only bear I'll see? A smudge sleeping
through our half hour horn, people yelling bye?

Split always, I question: is this enough?
It guards there in legend. Is this enough?
                        Is this enough?
                        Is this enough?
                        Is this enough?
                        Is this enough?
                        Is this enough?
                        Is this enough?

// **44**

I was there, almost crushed today between
the bulwark and a pallet of salt fish

on for Cartwright. The fore crane swung against
the wind to sudden stop nearly ending me there.

Back down in the hold, Lester examines
a shipped axe. *What a lovely axe,* he says,

and Brian grabs my shoulders, gives them a
shake. He says, *Your time's almost up, old buddy;*

won't be thinking about us boys on the boat.
He sighs, straps a pallet: *This woman I knows,*

I'd walk a mile on broken glass just to
hear her piss in a paint can over a long distance phone call,

and no better poem is said.
No better light: soft sun on steel bulkhead.

// **45**

An old passenger asks, *You Brent Chaulk's Boy?*
You looks just like he did. Don, neighbour of

my young father, lost his son to a car's
undertow. He was my uncle's best friend.

Don leaned, pointed to St. John Island over the rail,
That's Trout Head Cove, where your great grandfather

(and middle name) *Olin Chaulk, fished.*
My father knew him well. I knew him too.

Olin, who then fished through the hardships
of a family trapping for food, pelts, meat

bottled on the shelves. They were parents, looked
at their bodies each morning: please hold up.

I turned down so many visits to Mulligan
my dad stopped asking. Ashamed, I text him.

We need to plan a trip.

// **46**

Was brought once, four years old, to Mulligan,
to my grandparents' cabin to hunt ducks.

Poppy, my father, and dad's friend, Dave.
A photo of me and a rifle—ducks.

I missed my home, my high upstairs bedroom,
its window over prim afternoons and cars

through gentle screen; my mother, who moved tall
but bends—away.
                          Here, the smell of ringalls
from my old man at the woodstove too wild
a lunch. Caribou skillet fritters not

a new favourite of his boy, who rolls his
Gameboy's spent batteries like worry stones.

Bush neighbours hung their kills and catches from trees;
I busied myself with windowsill flies.

//   47

Last watch. I ask the captain where Mulligan is.
He points where Lake Melville forms a small bay,

starboard to us now, where our old cabin—
where it must have been that I was, through screams,

dragged down the cold beach by a sinewy
Labrador. Fred's black dog, never on leash,

hauled me by my shorts, the waistband stretched slack.
Swore I hated it here, would never come back.

On the chart, across the lake, I find old
Trout Head Cove. In behind where Olin fished

I read a shore named Port Disappointment,
abreast now. Maximus lowers a lifeboat;

I move to the window, see nothing there:
the ghosts of family, of language, a bear.

CROWN OF BROKEN BLOOD

for Bertha and Morris Chaulk

Maybe being mixed-race doesn't have to mean shaming myself out of my Indigeneity just because I wasn't raised in the culture: silently, safely watching from my whiteness as Native people around me suffered. Maybe it doesn't have to feel like forcing a smile for the same white people who continually gut my community and myself with dull blades. This is how I can decolonize my mind: by refusing the colonial narratives that try to keep me alienated from my own community.

– Alicia Elliott, *A Mind Spread Out On The Ground*

//

There is a problem here in telling how
I, confused, would move out of the sun, dark
all year but so dark in summer, they'd: *where from?
What are you?* Guesses thrown: *Dirty Mexican!
You look Asian.* Came home once to ask mom
why I'm the only black kid, me and Ralph—
Ralph's Filipino. Becomes in time a family
joke, like how Nanny said I looked just like
Tiger Woods, one of her favourite athletes.
I'm told later, older: *She would have never,
that's so funny, where'd you come up with that?*
The family laughs when we bring it up now.
I swore I remembered she— am told, Not;
I was young, confused for why I looked not—

//

I was young, confused for why I looked not
like those with clout, unable to transform
lack of light skin to positive presence, proud—
of something else. Sure, I must have been told,
but never in ways to kindle in kin.
Grasping ice-fished smelts, Nanny explained roe,
the strange orange tickle on my tongue: *some good,*
and komatik rides behind the snowmobile.
Besides, you looks it. I'm convinced that not
knowing how to say I'm Indigenous
means therein burns a lie closing in on
dim-lit embers capable of full fire;
else we'll lose those histories shamed away
and ourselves to that darkness, done.

//

And ourselves, to that darkness, done
little, indecisive, afraid of how—
Mike, doesn't your dad have Inuit status? Yes.
*Mike, you're not a full white person. Look at
you.* Well, then, look at me, stoned on the couch
in a panicked spell of: What if my work is bent
truth, my slow-woven identity cotton candy
before rain; *Whaddaya made'a, sugar?!*
Well my old man's from Goose Bay and he is—
Shhhh. S'okay. You're a smart person. You know
only what I've been told, gleaned together.
Am I the frozen arctic hare in my
dad's hands chasing my sister scared 'round chairs
or the dark-skinned boy on the couch, laughing?

//

Or the dark-skinned boy on the couch, laughing;
or my sister, bunny-lover, tough-willed;
or my Nan in her recliner, crossword
in lap in pursuit of the word, shaking
her head to say, *That's a sin, Brent, leave her
alone*; or my mother split between fun
and the duty to her own: *Ope! Haha;*
or Poppy in his recliner, big grin,
always in on the joke, chuckles out soft.
The freezer in the kitchen fills with char,
caribou, smelts, hot dogs, white bread, pot pies,
Big Land FM low on the radio:
call-ins for Labrador separatism,
local advertisements and new country.

//

Local advertisements and new country
become unbearable at times, as new country
proffers party and patriots, disregards
not its own: *And miles and miles of John Deere green,*
freedom far as I can see, which only sees
as far as privilege. Stolen land, treaties unfulfilled,
minorities un-free—who cold-yoked
this land to your fairy lights, dinner functions,
marketing campaigns to the marginal
good of whoever the fuck: *big smiles,*
post to Twitter!—

                    —Crises crush at my temples.
How do you say once without saying all?

//

How do you say once without saying all?
How do you write a poem of Natuashish,
of my first char caught off their rocks without
then Davis Inlet, the Mushuau Innu
nomadic until 1942 when, by the government,
forced to settle, forced to move to Nutak
far north, only to walk back home on foot;
without their history of strength squeezed against
missionaries, lost traditions, language, food;
without the RCMP poverty
tours for white Northern Ranger passengers;
without the youth crisis that hits media in 1993.
Six kids, ten to fourteen, inhale gas
on video, scream out: *I WANT TO DIE.*
Assholes on the crew call the place Nutville.

//

Asshholes on the crew call the place Nutville
and laugh, holding fast the ship lines on deck.
I say, *That's fucked up, there's reasons, just stop.*
Them: *Kids throw rocks at our heads when we dock.*
I tie my knot. *Doesn't matter. Just stop.*
They mostly do—when speaking to me. No victory here,
a deep-spliced thing is returned in long-bruised insults
to the crew—reciprocal exchange. A child, eight-ish, eyes me,
says slow as distance: *Fuck you, you fucking eskimo.*
The Innu are a land people, hunters
of caribou and catch char off their rocks.
I look at him, say, *It's okay, buddy,*
and he runs away, back to older kids
who meet down at the dock most times we come.

//

Who meets down at the dock most times we come?
Families, friends, folks to help guide their gear off;
more kids huddled in Hopedale, Nain. They hold hands,
sit on the wharfinger's hut, red-roofed, wave
as we leave. Their friends on deck yell long past
audibly, *Love yous, miss yous!* Laughing, they
hop excited in place, going to Goose Bay
or to visit family down in Hopedale.
We inhabit the ship together, all hope not
to sink together, navigate hidden shoals,
watch ice hit the hull. We push off together, too:
Innu, Inuit, white, at times nod hello
and sleep the lower decks, floor of the lounge.
We trust in the pair who steers the ship on.

//

We trust in the pair who steers the ship on.
I stand at the windows, watch moonlight milk
the horizon's dark waters, scan for lights,
land, rocks, and listen to mate's long stories
of *Used to this, that.* Now he buys and flip
cars off Kijiji, drawling his schemes as if
I were to do the same. *Quick cash, b'y!*
My infections change; I hear my g's drop,
having grown up 'round dad's accent, near
to Newfoundland's but unique to Goose and 'bouts.
Bits from up the North Coast too. When fired up
on the phone with his brother, Dave, he falls
into it, as I can, as confused by
the blend in my family as the other crew.

//

The blend in my family, as the other crew,
plays constant, constructs sides. Each time we dock
in Hopedale, I keep a close eye out for
Amos Semigak, an Inuk carver.
Always in hoodie, with backpack, he brings
a week's carvings: serpentine ulus, inuksuks,
a great bulbous nanuk I bought and brought home.
One day Amos gives Terry an eagle—commissioned.
Terry laughs, *This here eagle looks more like
a seagull!* So Amos grabs it, stomps up
the gangway, and chucks it in flight high out
to sink in dark harbour waters. Amos spits
and tears off. Terry's says, *He's crazy, drunk,*
not the artist you'd expect from first look.

//

Not the artist you'd expect from first look,
I spur work but stall, still haunted by problems
of position, of identity carved
from hockey in suburb-dusk that pretended
whiteness many times passed down. As was my
skin: darker. I heard Nanny said she'd get
teased by all her brothers for looking most—
big round face, light brown skin: *Our adopted
Eskimo sister,* they'd taunt, pretending
their own history away. Shame is bore on down
and teaches Goose Bay through a fractured lens.
Some drunk Indians, I'd hear twisting my
stomach's muscles. It was always known but
mapped back later, or else I never asked.

//

Mapped back later or else I never asked,
or how for years my family told stories
of where from and what's Labrador culture,
but race was mostly unspoken. I was
not taught pride. I avoided the sun
that darkens, feeling a natural drive build
according to forces I couldn't understand.
I hid difference and did disservice
to my family, sister, dad who shone proud
when I read "The Canada Goose"
at *Best Canadian Poetry*'s launch.
Was this an honest deep-dredging, a poem of
our own? *Oh my god, I think your dad was crying.*
I wonder how much more I could do for ours.

//

I wonder how much more I could do for ours,
a blend of peoples not uncommon to
Labrador, of families' unrecorded
mixings, of learned denials toward whiteness
that, alongside Indigenous pieces
are themselves passed down. I remember
how brown-purple my Nan's bare lips were.
Where they get the caribou for ringalls?
I asked Mom. *The community gives some
each season to elders.* Poppy didn't hunt
no longer, and I can no longer learn
the skills he had but those passed through my father.
We need to plan a trip. Together, there,
to learn we are, even if not full blood.

//

To learn we are, even if not full blood
bucks the project deep-built to disappear.
I did fade. Grown up muddled, I silenced
myself, watched my white friends on Instagram
post solidarity with Grassy Narrows,
Attawapiskat, Wet'suwet'en land,
while I stalled: who am I to get involved?
Vulnerable to questions, I feared them.
I feared my voice put out there be taken
as pretending my way into a conversation
in which I didn't belong. Shakily
on soft ground, my mix of bloods hot,
I feared what would happen if I spoke. Now
I fear too much could be lost if I don't.

//

I fear too much could be lost if I don't,
too many pinned by the colonial
hopes to shame mixed identities toward white,
toward going about a life not bothering.
But I've found ground that smells of bilge and char
where old Mokami and Mulligan grace
our distance. My father is crying, bears
losses: his father, culture, stories passed.
I'm here too. I fear still and stall sometimes,
but work toward speaking for my family, for
those who learned away from what we now hold
proud. My sister Marissa's with us. We
never quite know the way to say it right.
There is a problem too in telling how.

//Acknowledgments

Sherry Chaulk, Brent Chaulk, Marissa Chaulk, and Jen Van Lankveld, who have always supported me without pause. Theresa Mullin for love, emotional labour, and for continuously creating a home for us. Zane Koss for whom I have created more .docx files than what makes good sense – your friendship, edits, and insights mean the globe to me, bud. Emma Healey is a forever friend (back at you, finally). Maddy and Mikayla Van Lankveld are my impressive nieces. My grandparents are Bertha and Morris Chaulk, and Shirley and Norman Dugal, and I will forever regret all of the things they could have taught me if I were to have asked.

Thank you to the people of Nunatsiavut, Natuashish, and Labrador who spent time with me and helped me feel any amount of connection to the land, communities, and history. Thank you to all the crew of the M/V *Northern Ranger*, including Captain Paul Rogers, Terry Porter, Lester Burden, Darren Randell, Eric Sonny Lane, Ryan Pottle, Brian Ford, Randy Winters, and Scott Chant. Gratitude to the M/V *Visten* crew, from whom I learned when I was at my greenest.

Jeremy Luke Hill for your patience and commitment to Guelph's arts community. Shane Neilson for the lesson in clarity. Gordon Hill Press for all of your time, work, and trust.

Versions of poems 4, 6, and 8 were published as "Solo," "Cosmos," and "Palaeontologist" by *filling Station*. Versions of 24 and 25 were published as "Constellation" and "The Prank" by *Matrix*. Appreciation to all the folks there, respectively.

The following poems use material from these sources:

10 – "I hunt among stones" is from "The Kingfisher" by Charles Olson.

28 – The entire poem consists of the inscription on George Cartwright's memorial in one of the graveyards of Cartwright, NL.

41 – "A fisherman works without reference/ to that difference" is from "Maximus, to Gloucester, Sunday, July 19" by Charles Olson, *The Maximus Poems*; and "First men in it, the leaders, explorers were WORKERS" is from *Call me Ishmael* by Charles Olson, section entitled "what lies under".

44 – "walk a mile on broken glass..." is credited to Brian Ford, bosun of the M/V *Northern Ranger*, 2013.

// About the Author

Mike Chaulk lives in Guelph, Ontario, where he drives trucks full of beer for a living. His work has appeared or is forthcoming in *Best Canadian Poetry 2018, The Malahat Review, Arc Poetry Magazine, The Puritan, PRISM: international,* and *filling Station,* among other places. In 2015, Chaulk co-founded &, collective, an experimental poetry collective in Guelph, with whom he published two group chapbooks (*&, 1: works by &, collective,* self-published, and *&, 2: this happened to one of us,* Publication Studio Guelph). He has worked as a seaman in Labrador, Sweden, and Wales, and previously lived in Montreal for five years where he punched time as the Associate Poetry Editor of *The Incongruous Quarterly* as well as the Editor-in-Chief of *The Void Magazine* at Concordia University. He now spends a good deal of time walking his dog in the woods.